PASSING THE MIC

"Supporting DC SCORES has been a true highlight of my career. These poet-athletes have opened my eyes to so much, and have even pushed me outside of my own comfort zone and onto the poetry stage on at least one occasion! There's no better way to understand the hopes, fears, and dreams of kids than through their own words, so this is a treasure trove of knowledge that I hope everybody will pick up."

ASHLEY HATCH, Washington Spirit & US Women's National Team

—

"When I founded DC SCORES in 1994, I never imagined the tremendous impact our organization would have. This anthology is a testament to thousands of dedicated DC SCORES coaches, staff, and poet-athletes and the incredible program they built in the District. These poems are a beautiful portrait of a city seen through the eyes of its young people and teach us that we can all create change by using the power of imagination, community, and collective voice. I'm inspired in my own daily life by the writing on these pages."

JULIE KENNEDY, founder of DC SCORES

—

"In my entire career as a player and coach for D.C. United, I rarely missed a DC SCORES poetry slam. I loved them. I can relate on a personal level to the need to express yourself both physically and creatively, and I was always so grateful to know an organization in my city provided that for so many kids. I hope folks will pick up this book and learn from these poet-athletes, and support them for the next 30 years and beyond."

BEN OLSEN, former D.C. United coach and player

—

"Soccer has a unique power to connect, inspire, and build communities. It brings people together from all walks of life, creating bonds that go beyond the game. It has been a tremendous privilege to witness firsthand the impact DC SCORES has had in our community by using soccer to empower youth, foster confidence, and create opportunities for the next generation."

BRIANA SCURRY, legendary US Women's National Team Goalkeeper

Copyright © 2025 DC SCORES
First published 2025 by Shout Mouse Press

ISBN: 978-1-950807-84-0

Printed with permission from the authors.

All rights reserved.

Design by Amber Colleran

SHOUT MOUSE PRESS is a nonprofit organization that supports the creation and publication of diverse books by young people for young people. Learn more and see our full catalog at shoutmousepress.org

Shout Mouse Press
1638 R Street NW, Suite 218
Washington, DC 20009

For information about special discounts and bulk purchases, please contact Shout Mouse Press sales at 240-772-1545 or orders@shoutmousepress.org

PASSING THE MIC

BUILDING A POET-ATHLETE CITY

BY THE YOUNG POETS OF DC SCORES

CONTENTS

FOREWORD: *By Charity Blackwell*...**XI**
INTRODUCTION: *By Tatiana Figueroa Ramírez*..**1**
   OUR NEIGHBORHOOD: *Boone Elementary School | 2021* **5**

MAKING HISTORY **7**
   TO THE ONES WE LOVE: *By the Poet-Athletes from CW Harris Elementary School*....**9**
   UNTITLED: *By Erika J.* **10**
   THE UNBELIEVABLY BEAUTIFUL SUNRISE AND SUNSET:
      Barbara S., Naye' M., and Tiffany P. **11**
   WHAT DOES IT MEAN TO BE BLACK?: *By Antoine W.*............................**12**
   BREAKING THE CHAINS: *By Jalia C.* **14**
   VIRTUAL LEARNING BLUES: *By the Poet-Athletes from Boone Elementary School*....**15**
   OUR HISTORY IN SIMILES: *By the Poet-Athletes from Kimball Elementary School* ...**16**
   W.O.W. (WOMEN OF WORTH):
      By the Poet-Athletes from LaSalle-Backus Elementary School **17**
   OH, BUT WHY? (A TRIBUTE TO YAFET):
      By the Poet-Athletes from Barnard Elementary School **19**
   UNTITLED: *By the Poet-Athletes from Boone Elementary School* **20**
   A CRYING NIGHT: *By Kevin C.* **20**
   THE HISTORY OF BLACK CULTURE: *By the Poet-Athletes from Hart Middle School*....**21**
   CHINO: *By Brenda G.* **23**
   I REMEMBER MARY JANE: *By Angie R*..**24**
   UNTITLED: *By the Poet-Athletes from John Francis Education Campus* **26**

SPEAKING TRUTH **27**
   OUR COLORS OF EMOTION: *By the Poet-Athletes from Kimball Elementary School*..**28**
   TODAY MY NAME IS: *By Marcus G.* **29**
   MY TIME OF SORROW: *By Saba A.* **30**

PURE LOVE: *By Aniyah W.*	**31**
MY COMMUNITY: *By Shaun R.*	**32**
I AM: *By Miracle B.*	**33**
TODAY MY NAME IS....: *By Daniela S.*	**34**
I'M AFRAID: *By Ceila F.*	**35**
THE BEAT: *By Jason U.*	**36**
MY LATINA POEM: *By Kimberly S.*	**37**
INSECURITIES: *By the Poet-Athletes from Barnard Elementary School*	**38**
UNTITLED: *By the Poet-Athletes from Hart Middle School.*	**40**
WHY JUDGE?: *By Jerry C.*	**41**
THE YO-YO: *By Janeese L.*	**42**
AIN'T I A PERSON?: *By the Poet-Athletes from The Sojourner Truth School*	**42**
DEAR BLACK GIRL: *By the Poet-Athletes from Washington School for Girls*	**44**
HEY MAMA: *By Keyshawn, Navah, and La'Dae*	**45**
UNTITLED: *By the Poet-Athletes from Brookland Middle School*	**47**
MOTH: *By the Poet-Athletes from HD Cooke Elementary School*	**48**
I AM DC (THE CITY'S NEW PRINCESS): *By Toria L.*	**49**
ONE TEAM, ONE SCHOOL, ONE VOICE: *By the Poet-Athletes from Thomas Elementary School*	**50**
I HAVE THE RIGHT: *By Keshly A.*	**52**
I AM GIRL: *By Mariah P.*	**53**
ART : *By Athzyri H.*	**54**
POLITICAL DECISIONS: *By Kayla N..*	**55**
THAT AIN'T GANGSTA: *By the Poet-Athletes from Houston Elementary School*	**56**
BEING A GIRL: *By the Poet-Athletes from Excel Academy.*	**58**
COURAGE: *By the Poet-Athletes from Marie Reed Elementary School*	**60**
CROWN: *By the Poet-Athletes from Imagine Hope—Lamond.*	**62**
UNTITLED: *By the Poet-Athletes from Amidon-Bowen Elementary School*	**63**
LIKE: *By the Poet-Athletes from KIPP DC: AIM Academy*	**64**
WE ARE: *By the Poet-Athletes from Shirley Chisholm Elementary School.*	**65**
POWER OF YOUR SMILE: *By Jaiden R.*	**67**
SHINING BRIGHT: *By the Poet-Athletes from Powell Elementary School*	**68**

COPS AND THE PEOPLE: *By Da'Niya A.* **69**
KINDNESS IN THE WORLD: *By the Poet-Athletes from Thomson Elementary School* **70**
WE CAN INSPIRE: *By the Poet-Athletes from Tubman Elementary School* **71**

BECOMING VISIONARIES **73**
LET'S ALL SAVE THE WORLD TOGETHER: *By Jasia S.* **74**
MY DREAM: *By Jennifer P* **75**
IN MY PERFECT WORLD…: *By Xiu Qi C.* **76**
RECIPE FOR PEACE: *By the Poet-Athletes from Noyes Education Campus* **77**
THE SKY IS THE LIMIT: *By A'Dora W.* **78**
I HAVE THE POTENTIAL:
   By the Poet-Athletes from Arts & Technology Academy **79**
I WISH I WAS A WISHING WELL: *By Keiry A.* **80**
I WISH: *By Eriq B.* **81**
LET'S HAVE A FREE WORLD: *By Marshae J.* **82**
I'M DREAMING: *By the Poet-Athletes from Burrville Elementary School* **83**
THE POWER IN ME: *By the Poet-Athletes from Marie Reed Elementary School* **84**
MY DREAM: *Saba A.* **85**
A RECIPE FOR A GREAT AMERICA:
   By the Poet-Athletes from LaSalle-Backus Education Campus **86**
MY MAGICAL WORLD: *By Ashley R.* **87**
JUST IMAGINE: *By the Poet-Athletes from Raymond Education Campus* **88**
MARKING THE FUTURE: *By the Poet-Athletes from Bancroft Elementary School* ... **89**
PEOPLE OF THE WORLD: *By the Poet-Athletes from Beers Elementary School* **90**
SAVING OUR GENERATION: *By the Poet-Athletes from Imagine Hope—Tolson* **91**
WE ARE THE FUTURE: *By the Poet-Athletes from Seaton Elementary School* **92**
DREAMS: *By the Poet-Athletes from Walker Jones Education Campus* **93**

AFTERWORD: *by Clint Smith* **95**

FOREWORD

BY CHARITY BLACKWELL
CHIEF OF CULTURE AND ARTS, DC SCORES

POETRY IS THE RHYTHM of the heart, the anthem of dreams, and the unyielding voice of resilience. It is where truths are told and where power is reclaimed. For 30 years, DC SCORES has been a staple of poetry in the District, channeling the voices of youth into verses that transcend generations. Our poet-athletes have written themselves into history—page by page, stanza by stanza, word by word.

This anthology is not just a celebration of three decades of creativity and courage; it is a testament to the unshakable spirit of our young leaders. These are not merely poems; they are declarations of identity, courage, and hope. They tackle the struggles of virtual learning, the pain of loss, the fight for justice, and the celebration of community. They dream big, imagine vividly, and inspire deeply.

Within these pages, you will meet voices that reflect the soul of a city—diverse, bold, and unapologetic. You will witness the brilliance of poet-athletes whose words break barriers and build bridges. From the joy of playing soccer to the dreams of a brighter future, these poems remind us that every child's story matters and that their voices can change the world.

As the Chief of Culture and Arts, I am honored to stand beside our poet-athletes, who remind us that art is activism and storytelling is liberation. Let this collection inspire you as it has inspired me—to listen more, to dream boldly, and to champion the voices of the next generation.

This anthology marks 30 years of creating a space where every child can say, "I am seen, I am heard, and I am powerful." Here's to 30 more years of amplifying the voices that shape our world.

CHARITY BLACKWELL
CHIEF OF CULTURE AND ARTS, **DC SCORES**

INTRODUCTION

BY TATIANA FIGUEROA RAMÍREZ

DC SCORES was founded 30 years ago in 1994 at Marie Reed Elementary School by teacher Julie Kennedy who saw the need for afterschool activities for her students. Soccer, poetry, and service learning were intertwined into one program with the mission of empowering DC youth to lead healthy lives with the confidence to know the difference they can make in this world. This formed the birth of the poet-athlete. Youth who embody taking care of the whole self—physically, mentally, and emotionally—to emerge as leaders of their community. Undoubtedly, poetry has stood out as the most impactful platform for our youth to care for their mental and emotional health, to express themselves freely, and be heard authentically.

Every year, our poet-athletes work through our *Power of Poetry* and *Speak Up, Write Now* poetry curricula alongside teachers who serve as writing coaches to create their original poems, reflecting their very real lived experiences and unique perspectives of the world. Throughout the years, DC SCORES has expanded its poetry programming to culminate with annual poetry slams, include middle schools, and offer opportunities to alumni through Youth WORD Project where poet-athletes with a particular interest and talent for poetry are able to work closely with award-winning poets and perform at premier venues, such as the National Museum of African American History.

Our poet-athletes now come from 7 of DC's 8 wards and have written thousands of poems throughout the years to create the dream of Poet-Athlete City. Poet-Athlete City is the idea that every youth who needs it will have access to our free programming, allowing them to engage in sports and formative poetry activities to build their holistic health and confidence. With out-of-school time support at risk, it is more important than ever to emphasize the necessity for DC SCORES programming. The hours of 2pm-6pm are the most dangerous time of the day for our youth, so providing accessible, youth-centric programming is critical to ensuring the safety and continued development of our young people.

In 2024, DC SCORES partnered with the like-minded nonprofit Shout Mouse Press to develop the concept for a poetry anthology, putting youth at the center to celebrate 30 years of amplifying kids' voices. This anthology brings together just a fraction of our youth's work to highlight how poet-athletes are historians, storytellers, visionaries, diverse with unique perspectives and living shared experiences that transcend three decades. They are the brave voices that carry across years and place to say out loud what many of us think and feel.

In a workshop hosted by Shout Mouse Press, a group of Youth WORD Project poet-athletes came together to discuss their intention for this collection of poetry. The sentiments of not feeling alone, being heard, being seen, and inspiring others were the themes our youth determined should be the focus of this book. In these poems, our hope is that our poet-athletes past, present, and future can see themselves reflected to understand the power they wield with their words. The power they can pass on to the next generation of poet-athletes.

Passing the Mic shows the world what a Poet-Athlete City can look, feel, and sound like. Poet-athletes make history by documenting what they have lived, felt, and witnessed. From the pandemic to elections, poet-athletes were there and they remind us of their irreplaceable role as documentarians. Poet-athletes speak truth to immortalize the now they live and embody. From self-affirmations to celebrating their community, poet-athletes use language to widen the mirrors they hold up to create the reflections most books lack. Poet-athletes become visionaries by sharing their hopes, dreams, and imagined futures. From ending gun violence to becoming president, poet-athletes see no limits for themselves, and why should they?

OUR NEIGHBORHOOD

BY THE POET-ATHLETES FROM
BOONE ELEMENTARY SCHOOL | 2021

Have you been to DC lately?
Take a walk with me
Just across the school, someone got shot
A soul was taken, a dream was stopped.
Have you been to DC lately?
From our classroom window, we can see the capital
Where your skin no matter the cause decides
if you're a protestor or an unamerican criminal
Have you been to DC lately?
A place of lightness and darkness
Liberty and justice for some
Carry-outs, laughter, and pain
Gogo music running through our veins
Have you been to DC lately?

Coming live from fox 5
We'd like to show some positive images of us
The joy that Big Mamas hugs brings
Our faces taking in the sun
Leaning back on a swing
We'd like to show some positive images of us
Coming live from fox 5
The laughter of joanin' in our crew
But nobody's mad because we all love you
We'd like to show some positive images of us
Playing soccer cheering on our team
Each day is an adventure, holding on to our dreams
Can you show some positive images of us?
Coming live from fox 5

MAKING HISTORY

TO THE ONES WE LOVE

BY THE POET-ATHLETES FROM
CW HARRIS ELEMENTARY SCHOOL | 2022

To the ones we love
and to the ones we lost.
You were so important to us,
you had no cost.

We will miss you so
and always wonder why you, of all people,
were chosen to go.

Brothers, sisters and all family and friends
will have to go one day.
We just don't know when, it all depends.

We must be kind to each other while we can
Find the simple joys to make us laugh.
Then spread positivity and Kindness to the world
on their behalf.

A message to our special ones who have passed on.
We hope you watch over us,
Just like you did when you were alive.
We promise to make you proud,
work hard, succeed, achieve and thrive.
All day baby!!!

UNTITLED

BY ERIKA J. | 2010
HOWARD ROAD ACADEMY

I remember
my grandma's hands felt
like scales on fish.
I remember
my 6th birthday when
I had a kitty cat parade.
I had a lot of fun.
I remember
my father treating
me nicely. I got
a Playstation 2 with lots of games and DVDs.
I remember
the dogs my next-door neighbor had
in Georgia. The smallest dog always jumping
on my grandfather.
I remember
my uncle's wedding.
It was at a fire station.
I ate a lot of food.
I remember
my 2nd birthday party. My grandma
sent me a lemon pound cake to school.

THE UNBELIEVABLY BEAUTIFUL SUNRISE AND SUNSET

BY BARBARA S., NAYE' M., AND TIFFANY P. | 1998
BOONE ELEMENTARY SCHOOL
(FORMERLY ORR ELEMENTARY SCHOOL)

The unbelievably beautiful sunrise started to turn black. The sun was starting to go down really quickly. It was just like another day had passed that morning

Then Tania started to cry because she was about to be late for school. It seemed that the day was going by really fast.

The next day she went back to the sunrise and sunset, but she did not hear its sweet voice or see the dancing. She ran home to tell her mother and father.

They told her they were sorry about the sunrise and sunset. They were sorry she would not hear the sweet voice and see the dancing.

The next day she walked to school. It was an ordinary day, but ever since then things have not been the same with the sunrise and sunset.

WHAT DOES IT MEAN TO BE BLACK?

BY ANTOINE W. | 2005
STANTON ELEMENTARY SCHOOL
SUMMER CAMP

What it means
to be Black is being
different
having your own style
Slavery is where our
great-great-grandparents were
Most people thinking
this our setback
Instead
it was the beginning
to great things happening

Black people have created
a lot of things
We revolutionized
the world of music
Hip Hop was just a thing we did on the block
We took it from the block
and brought
it to America Music saves
us
It is a way to express
our ways

Clothing is another way we
as Black people express
our beliefs
Clothing can tell
how we are feeling
that day or make
a statement
In many ways
we do things that express
our feelings towards being
African American.

Some things people can't take away from us
I love being Black!

BREAKING THE CHAINS

BY JALIA C. | 2017
WHITLOCK ELEMENTARY SCHOOL
(FORMERLY AITON ELEMENTARY SCHOOL)

Breaking the chains from the caucasian who taught me to read
to slaves who have been freed
while we asked "why me?"
to the north we wanted to flee
escapes we tried to make
we sung songs for god's sake
wanting to save the next generation
either life behind bars or planting crops while singing
chains we hear rattling and ringing
together
locking arms marching down streets
hoping one day to go home to start a career of our own
leaving tears of a heart and a soul
stories passed down about what we fought for
looking down at our rags as we could
and will be the generation to break the chains

VIRTUAL LEARNING BLUES

BY THE POET-ATHLETES FROM
BOONE ELEMENTARY SCHOOL | 2022

Let me paint the picture of what my days looked like
Virtual Learning Blues
All of us rushing to login after playing video games all night
Virtual Learning Blues
How can I focus when the smell of bacon is taking over the house
Virtual Learning Blues
I'll just turn my camera off and sneak off like a mouse
Virtual Learning Blues
Helloooo scholars are you there?
Virtual Learning Blues
I can tell my teacher's tired
because she turns off her camera too
This is what we call virtual learning blues

OUR HISTORY IN SIMILES

BY THE POET-ATHLETES FROM
KIMBALL ELEMENTARY SCHOOL | 2022

The history of our people is long like a never-ending ruler
Even though we don't get our props, Our culture and style has
    only made this nation cooler
From Africa to America our story is powerful like a tsunami wave
Our legacy runs so deep it can fill up the biggest cave
Barack Obama, Dr. King, and Me
I am what my ancestors always dreamed of when they
    became free.

Our hair shines more than the rising of the sun
Our crown represents our power and a new day begun
They call our hair dreadful, unruly, and wild
Then can someone please tell me why they stay copying our style?

Our melanin is the blueprint of where we came from
So keep your low expectations and your pity, because we don't
    need them

The different shades of our skin was the magic to our freedom

Our skin is like a full box of crayons... Or a pool of chocolate that
    glows under the light

Can't nobody tell me My black ain't beautiful (I know that's right)

W.O.W.
(WOMEN OF WORTH)

**BY THE POET-ATHLETES FROM
LASALLE-BACKUS ELEMENTARY SCHOOL | 2024**

Women are strong, women are brave,
Women have made strides they have paved.
We know who they are because history has brought us so far.
They work hard and they try their best,
Some women work tirelessly without any rest.
Women of worth, we honor you
For all that you have done and all that you will do.

Sonia Sotomayor is her name.
The first Latina Supreme Court Justice is her fame.

Mae Jemison, the first Black female to go into space.
The first to set the pace, so we recognize her face.

Michelle Obama, African American First Lady of our nation.
Wife, mother and a total inspiration.

Serena Williams, the G.O.A.T. of tennis.
Slams that ball from start to finish.

Malala Yousafzai fights for girls' education in Pakistan.
Nothing can stop her, not even the Taliban.

continued on page 18

continued from page 17

Amanda Gorman is the youngest poet to speak at a
   Presidential Inauguration.
Her poem, The Hill We Climb, was about our nation.

Ketanji Brown Jackson, first black woman to serve on the
   Supreme Court.
We saw her battles and how hard she fought.

Kamala Harris, first Black Vice President of our day.
She vows to put the people first in the USA.

We're so happy to have them on our Earth
These **BOLD** and **AWESOME** Women of Worth!

OH, BUT WHY? (A TRIBUTE TO YAFET)

BY THE POET-ATHLETES FROM BARNARD ELEMENTARY SCHOOL | 2019

We didn't see it coming, looking
forward to the first day of school.
Only to hear that life is so cruel.
Still in disbelief
and school hasn't been the same.
But we will forever cherish
the memories and honor your name.
The news of your passing left me distraught,
we'll never forget the lessons you taught.
You were smart, you were funny,
you were kind and caring. You were special
and not like the others.
One who had a passion for reading.
You were an amazing person, a friend, a comforter, a son,
"You were my brother from another mother"
I didn't even get to say goodbye.
Often catch myself asking WHY?
Why did it have to end this way?
**It's been a long day without you, my friend
And I'll tell you all about it when I see you again. **
Who's gonna look out for me and make sure I don't go astray?
I know you're up there watching over us all.
Waiting to pick us up when we fall.
Don't cry they say, but it's just not fair
when we just lost a Barnard Bear.
READ ON YAFET! WE MISS YOU!!!

UNTITLED

**BY THE POET-ATHLETES FROM
BOONE ELEMENTARY SCHOOL | 2019**

Children don't belong in cages
Children belong in classrooms
Reading books that take them to distant places
This is a place that some of them dream about
And now they roam about a cage
A place that they read about
But now it's no longer a place for dreamers who want better lives
Now you better think twice

A CRYING NIGHT

BY KEVIN CLARK | 1998
JC NALLE ELEMENTARY SCHOOL

One night my father and I
were coming out of the store when
my father got shot
in the arm. I ran
and told my grandmother about it.
She told me to lay down
and I cried myself to sleep.

THE HISTORY OF BLACK CULTURE

BY THE POET-ATHLETES FROM HART MIDDLE SCHOOL | 2019

It started with Harriet and the slave masters
then to Rosa and the bus.

White people couldn't suppress us.

Then it happened to Rodney
who was beaten so senseless
to Black people coming back so relentless.

Then all Black kids in school
started getting suspended.

Then it was Black vs. white
that caused a lot of drama.

Then the church bombing
that caused so much trauma.

To before a little girl died
her last word was mama.

Then with the Twin Towers
caused by Osama.

continued on page 21

continued from page 21

To Blacks getting their real first president
Obama.

With Blacks having all the power,
white people were scared
they would lose their power.

Becoming entrepreneurs and
opening up the doors
all Black-owned businesses
stacked up is 100 floors.

Now we have a lot of residents,
this is my perspective of Black Excellence.

CHINO

BY BRENDA G. | 2009
MACFARLAND MIDDLE SCHOOL

He was born
I was born
He walked
I walked
He smiled
I smiled
I turned 11
He turned 12
He breathed
I breathed
He ate
I ate
He had munchies
I had munchies
He got high
I was at home
He got stabbed
I wondered
He died
I cried.

I REMEMBER MARY JANE

BY ANGIE R. | 2019
TUBMAN ELEMENTARY SCHOOL

Let me tell you about my friend Mary Jane,
She was sweet and caring, and she had a big brain.

Every single day she made us laugh,
If you were feeling small she'd make you feel as tall as a giraffe.

MJ loved to talk about farts
But she also loved to make beautiful art.

This girl was extremely sassy!
But also she was very classy.

MJ was the coolest nerd you could ever meet,
Every single day she surprised her teacher, Ms. Wheat.

Mary Jane loved to sing every day
In her head, she thought she was Beyoncé.

If you were ever feeling sad, MJ could make you smile.
Lip gloss, headbands, fake glasses and glitter were MJ's
    signature style.

continued on page 25

continued from page 24

Pink, purple, rainbows and chips were some of MJ's
    favorite things.
So were unicorns, gel pens, her family, her friends, her school,
    and anything with bling.

I feel like everyone is lonely without her,
So we all have to support each other.

I wish I had the power to prevent her from dying,
I pray and I dream but still I am crying.

MJ, right now some days are hard to get through,
But for the rest of my life I will remember you.

UNTITLED

**BY THE POET-ATHLETES FROM
JOHN FRANCIS EDUCATION CAMPUS | 2024**

In halls once filled with laughter and light,
A shadow fell on that fateful night,
Parkland's peace shattered by a tragic cry,
As hearts were broken and questions why.

Young lives, with dreams yet to unfold,
Stolen in moments, stories unfold,
Bravery rose amidst the fear,
As heroes emerged, their courage clear.

A community mourns, united in pain,
Seeking solace, striving for change.
In memory of those who were taken too soon,
We vow to fight, their legacy our tune.

Survivors stand, their spirits strong,
Voices raised in a collective song.
Emma, David, and many more,
Turned their grief into a roar.

Demanding justice, pleading for peace,
Their fight for safety will never cease.
In classrooms, homes, and the public square,
Their message echoes everywhere.

For those who perished, we remember their names,
Their memories cherished, their lives not in vain.
From the ashes of sorrow, hope starts to rise,
In the hearts of the survivors, the future lies.

SPEAKING TRUTH

OUR COLORS OF EMOTION

**BY THE POET-ATHLETES FROM
KIMBALL ELEMENTARY SCHOOL | 2021**

Most people are limited to what their eyes can see,
But the color of my skin, doesn't define me,

My future is promising and paved with gold,
Like the crowns of my people before they were captured and sold,

Fierce as a bull, whose eyes locked on red,
Thick as the blood, that my ancestors shed,

Flawless and blue, like the cloudless summer skies,
Or the blues I may sing with tears in my eyes,

Focused on the green, not just for myself,
But the kind that feeds the family, that generational wealth,

We all play in purple, don't get lost in the haze,
If at first you slept on us, you'll leave out amazed,

Bright orange and yellow, like the flare of the sun,
Or the fire inside, that burns until we won,

What hides in the shadows, always comes to light,
There's more to us than black and white.

TODAY MY NAME IS

BY MARCUS G. | 2009
KELLY MILLER MIDDLE SCHOOL

Today my name is Albert Einstein
I feel like the smartest person in the world
I pretend that I know everything

Yesterday my name was Sherlock Holmes
I heard noise in my room
I found my brother in my room watching TV

Tomorrow my name will be forgetful boy
I will forget to do my homework
I will remember that I forgot to do my homework

MY TIME OF SORROW

BY SABA A. | 2009
MACFARLAND MIDDLE SCHOOL

I hear the words
Over and over again
"He is dead, He is dead."
I felt my heart shatter into pieces
I thought to myself this can't be true
This can't happen to me
I fell to the ground
With lightning through my mind
My body shook like thunder
My tears dropped to the ground
As if houses were flooding
I thought in my mind,
"This is my moment of sorrow."

PURE LOVE

BY ANIYAH W. | 2011
NOYES EDUCATION CAMPUS

My heart shimmers.
I fall in love
My heart is breaking,
Of lakes.
I am in love,
While swans flow,
My love,
A mystery as I go on.
Where is he
This is my best friend
My best friend's name is Joredine
He is not here today.
He is gone.
I end in tears
Swans turn into dust
The river is no longer fast,
It is slow.
The animals look sad, I walk through the park.
They Run,
Looks like God's Tears
It Starts all over again.

MY COMMUNITY

BY SHAUN R. | 2011
LINCOLN MIDDLE SCHOOL

I smell trash
I smell dirt
I smell people
They're getting hurt

People lie
People cheat
Blood is at their feet

The innocent are blamed
When hands aren't tamed
Will we ever be free
Of the tyranny
Of the guilty

I AM

BY MIRACLE B. | 2011
JEFFERSON MIDDLE SCHOOL

I am a monkey in the moonlight, swinging limb to limb.
I am a converse in the horizon with no destination in mind.
I am outgoing, outspoken, and outstanding.
I am a rock star on a stage in front of a million people,
screaming my name.
I am not careless.
I am not annoying.
I am not wild.
I am an untamed specimen, who's wriggling under a microscope.
I am a book on the bookshelf, waiting to be read.
I am a pen, waiting to be uncapped.
I am Nick Jonas with my green guitar.
I am David Beckham with my soccer ball.
I am Orlando Bloom with my acting skills, but most of all,
I AM ME!

TODAY MY NAME IS....

BY DANIELA S. | 2009-2010
HD COOKE ELEMENTARY SCHOOL

Today my name is revolution
I feel like a screaming prisoner
I pretend to be a person I'm not

Yesterday my name was depressed
I heard about people starving and dying
I found no more money in my wallet

Tomorrow my name will be clock
I will forget that there is a such thing as life
I will remember that the only thing I can do is
go through time not knowing who I am

I'M AFRAID

BY CEILA F. | 2004
BRIGHTWOOD ELEMENTARY SCHOOL

I'm afraid of God.
I'm afraid of life.
I'm afraid to grow up.
I'm afraid of people being jealous.
I'm afraid of people hating.
I'm afraid to have a kid.
I'm afraid to die, which I know every thought process.
I'm afraid of the devil which I think I'm not supposed to.
When I'm bigger, I hope I'm not afraid of all these things.

THE BEAT

BY JASON U. | 2011
TUBMAN ELEMENTARY SCHOOL

While I was in the hallway
there was a janitor
dancing to the beat.
And I wondered
why she likes it so much.
She was sweeping
and I got swept
into the room.
I was dust
along with dirt.

MY LATINA POEM

BY KIMBERLY S. | 2018
NEVAL THOMAS ELEMENTARY

Some people think it's easy to be Latina
Like we just eat Chipotle or Taco Bell 24/7
But no, mi madre y mi abuelita make pupusas, tamales,
elote loco, flan y taquiitos.
In the kitchen, I am learning how to cook while listening
to stories about my family's history.
Some people think it's easy to be Latina but it's not.
Our President won't let Hispanic people
have their sueño Americano.
I get bullied for the color of my skin.
I get depressed and I don't know what to do so I cry.
But as a Latina, I have to be powerful.
I wear the colors of my flag with pride.
Someone told me, "tú mi corazón late"
Be confident, the world is fearful of the confident.
As a Salvadoran American Latina,
I filled with confidence and pride.
Con amor y respect por los demás.
I am a beautiful Latina!
Soy una bella Latina!

INSECURITIES

BY THE POET-ATHLETES FROM BARNARD ELEMENTARY SCHOOL | 2021

What do insecurities really mean?
Is it something that is seen?
Can you touch it?
How does it feel?
Is it something that is real?
I'm not sure I can understand the big deal.

Insecurities are something I have which I do not want.
It makes me sad, and it is not fun.
When I look at the magazines the models are pretty
and so brave to show themselves,
then I look in the mirror and what do I see? Ears like an elf.
My teeth start to spread and my tears to shed.
My hair disappears and then I start to tear.

Insecurities, Insecurities, what should I do?
The voices in my head call me a fool.
Insecurities, Insecurities please go away!
I do not want to shed another tear today.

I feel all twisted up inside. I can run but I can't hide
From the things I think about myself,
my nose is too big, my eyes are too small,
or my body isn't good enough.
I try to love myself, but I cannot.
How is everyone so attractive and I am not?

continued on page 38

continued from page 38

"Your teeth are messed up," "your clothes are cheap,"
"You need to lose some weight,"
All my insecurities come from this evil hate.
But I know that no one is perfect, I'm learning every day,
I am a work in progress, no matter what people say.
"YASSSS Queen," "You are so beautiful," "You are such a vibe!!!"
These are the kind words that build my self-pride.
Insecurities, Insecurities, please give it a rest!
No, I am not perfect, but I am a work in progress!

UNTITLED

BY THE POET-ATHLETES FROM
HART MIDDLE SCHOOL | 2021

Let the bruises on your body that fade or stay as scars
be a reminder that EVERYBODY has a story.
We all have good days and bad days and we all go through something
whether physically or emotionally.
No matter young or old, with that in mind... I want you to know
You should Never judge someone you DON'T know
because we ALL go through something.

Let the bruises remind you of how you got hurt.
Let the screaming remind you of why you were angry.
Let the crying remind you of why you were sad.
Let the smile remind you of why you were happy.
Let the laugh remind you of JOY.

Let love remind you of all these things
and let it be a healing process for you.
Most importantly, let the sadness be a process of learning
that crying and screaming is IMPORTANT.
You are allowed to FEEL.
Let that breakdown remind you
that we are ALL humans, because whether we try to hide it or not
WE FEEL...

WHY JUDGE?

BY JERRY C. | 2021
KIMBALL ELEMENTARY SCHOOL

Why Judge?
Is it the color of my skin?... the clothes that I wear?
My family? My friends? The kinks in my hair?

Why Judge?
Is it because I'm a Prince? The heir to the throne?
With skill, swag, and the gift of gab, someone like you clearly doesn't own?

Why Judge?
Is it cause I'm from a city they wanna mute and silence, labeled by endless slander?
Because I'd prefer the tune of BYB and Big G, to star and spangle my banner?

Why Judge?
Is it because I'm careful with my digital footprint? I don't be wildin' on Instagram.
Or that my family hold me down through whatever? Step outta line and they'll go Insta-ham!

Why Judge?
Is it because I set the table, And gave you gems while only 10 years old?
Or because now you got that ITIS, from this food I just fed your soul!

THE YO-YO

BY JANEESE L. | 1998
RUDOLPH ELEMENTARY SCHOOL

It goes up and down, round and round till it touches the ground.
It can come in red, yellow, black or green.
So spin it fast not slow, it may turn colors.
You never know.

AIN'T I A PERSON?

**BY THE POET-ATHLETES FROM
THE SOJOURNER TRUTH SCHOOL | 2021**

Ain't I a Person?
Whose voice is special?
Whose voice is loved?

Ain't I a person?
Whose voice can go beyond and above?
Whose voice is strong?

Ain't I a person?
Whose voice is strong enough to be heard?

continued on page 42

continued from page 42

Ain't I a person?
Whose beautiful black voice can make an impression
    on this world?

With the ability to cause earthquakes
And break down your beliefs and stigmas.
My voice represents years of fighting
I will not be silenced

From Rosa Parks
To Sojourner Truth
You could not silence my voice with a noose

My voice is proof.
That black will always be beautiful
Never shaken

Ain't I a person
Strong enough to change the universe and move mountains.

My black is beautiful
And so is our voices.

DEAR BLACK GIRL

BY THE POET-ATHLETES FROM WASHINGTON SCHOOL FOR GIRLS | 2021

Dear black girl
We are magical, yes we are we
We are not just smart. We think from the heart

Dear black girl
Our skin color is powerful it really is
Take a look and you'll see how special it is

Dear black girl
Our voice is powerful. It should be heard
Black girls are intelligent so we like to learn

Dear black girl
We make a difference no one can touch
And like I said earlier black girls are not just smart
We grow up to be true to who we are

Dear black girl
We are black,
We are proud
And we stand out in front of the crowd

That's why

BLACK GIRLS ROCK

HEY MAMA

BY KEYSHAWN T., NA'VAH W., AND LA'DAE A. | 2024
STANTON ELEMENTARY SCHOOL

My mom loves me, and you want to know how I know?
It's not just good luck
Or because she buys me robux... which I love.
My mom cooks for me and tries her hardest to keep a roof over our heads.
And make sure we have clean rooms and beds.
My mom tries hard putting food in the fridge and the freezer.
And I try to do my best and please her.
But not everyone has a mom like I do,
With tons of love and care.
Some moms are not here but I am willing to share.
I know, not having a mom can be tough
and it feels like some things come to an end.
But you know who can tell you best? My friends.

If my mom was still here, everything would be perfect.
We would get our hair and nails done and get new outfits.
I remember her teaching me how important it was to save.
And how much fun we would have on our coin star visit days.
She would let me get everything I wanted
And I even got things for her,
I am trying to explain just how much I miss her.
I loved our pep talks and, even when we didn't have much,
I told her it would get better.
Sadly, she won't get to hear my dear mom letter.

continued on page 46

continued from page 45

I hate that she got breast cancer and got sick.
But her memories, loves, hugs, and kisses will always stick…
In my heart.

My mom, I love my mom, she did everything for me.
She spoiled me and gave me the attention I needed.
She's gone.
And it's okay because I try to stay strong.
I miss my mom and love her so much.
Her kisses, her tickles, and her touch.
I remember she used to play with me and my sister.
Until this day, I really miss her.
So, to my mom, here is a poem I wrote for you.
Until this day, I'm sad
It went from the three of us to two.

UNTITLED

BY THE POET-ATHLETES FROM BROOKLAND MIDDLE SCHOOL | 2022

I just want to help you laugh,
Listen to the pure essence of your soul.
I just want to help you smile,
Watch those bright eyes sparkle and glow.
I just want to help you sleep,
Dream of endless possibilities and peace.
I just want to make you cry,
Let go of all the hurt inside.
I just want to take your hand,
overlapping fingers to help you understand.
I just want to hold you close.
You are safe – release those heavy hidden stones.
I just want to let you know that I am here.

MOTH

BY THE POET-ATHLETES FROM
HD COOKE ELEMENTARY SCHOOL | 2014

I've always been jealous of a moth.
Yes.
A moth.
Because people just leave them alone.
They just let them fly on their own.

Who pays attention to that ugly thing?
But it's the freest of creatures.
It flutters its wings
so independently
And nobody seems to care.

I AM DC (THE CITY'S NEW PRINCESS)

BY TORIA L. | 2022
KIMBALL ELEMENTARY SCHOOL

CHOCOLATE CITY, that's the place I call home,
That Capitol siege was cute, but try that mess on the block that my homies roam,
You take us out in dozens, but your tactics only make us stronger,
And SLIM I KNOW MY RIGHTS, and what you doing can't get no wronger!
Distance learning was a disaster!!! Tell me again... where did you put that money?
Because the poor got poorer and the rich look richer, Hmmm... ain't that funny,
A lot around here is changing, but I have a feeling it the change ain't for me,
You can try to erase the hoods in the city but the fact remains, "I AM DC!!!"

ONE TEAM, ONE SCHOOL, ONE VOICE

BY THE POET-ATHLETES FROM THOMAS ELEMENTARY SCHOOL | 2014

We are a Team, a school and a community of change.
When you hear us talk, we talk about love, change and
    becoming a family.

When my school came to Thomas,
I was nervous, who would be there?
I was scared, would I have friends?
I am smart, how would the teachers know?
My heart pounded as I got on the bus,
My eyes watered as we drove away from my old school,
My life changed but Why?

I am Trayvon, I am Michael, I am Jayden.
Bang, Bang our community isn't safe.
I want UNITY, for my school and my community.
I want people to know I have potential.
I want people to know I have a dream.
I want people to believe in me.
I want people to think about their choices.
I want people to care about what happens to me.
I want people to know that at Thomas, I am someone.
Someone with thoughts, a choice and a dream.

continued on page 50

continued from page 50

My school, it is an important place to be.
My school it is where children laugh, play and learn.
I am smart because of my school.
When I graduate, I am going to thank Neval Thomas.
We have to work hard and get smarter.
Our teachers, keep us trying to do more, get back on
  point and work hard.
We are the best, better than the rest at Neval Thomas.

We are Thomas, We are Family.
We care when someone gets hurt.
We miss Jayden and are waiting for him to come back.
He is strong, We are strong.
Jayden will return the friend, we miss every day.

Our Thomas School Family,
Ask that you think,
Put down your weapons,
Use your voice, Speak Loudly,
Shout to bring Change About.

I HAVE THE RIGHT

BY KESHLY A. | 2015
BANCROFT ELEMENTARY SCHOOL

I am a child with eyes, a mouth, and a powerful voice.
I have the right to be a child,
I have the right to live under a peaceful roof,
I have the right.
I have the right to go to school,
I have the right to an education
whether I am Hispanic, Black, White, Short, Tall, Smart, or not.
I have the right to envision a bright future,
I have the right to create, imagine, and express my emotions,
I Have the Right.

I AM GIRL

BY MARIAH P.
ELIOT-HINE MIDDLE SCHOOL

From the time I was born, I was born with grace.
I was born with the smile of my ancestors on my face.
I feel beauty on the outside and beauty within.
From the first time I saw my mother's eyes, I was filled with pride.
    That built the love inside that will never die.
My existence is she. She is me.
And we are girls.
The pride of the world
In us there is life. Not death.
I am a girl. A jewel to the world.
I should be respected as such.
I am a girl that is too much.

ART

BY ATHZYRI H. | 2017
TUBMAN ELEMENTARY SCHOOL

Amazing
Be creative
Colors
Drawing
Elegance
Frees my mind
Great start to my day
How I learn about myself
I am an artist
Just see what happens
Know your technique
Love what you make
Markers and messes
Need more time
Original
Paint
Quiet time
Relaxing
Special
Teachers help me
Uniting us all with artwork
Very magical
What I love
Xtra peaceful
You should try it
Zoom in

POLITICAL DECISIONS

KAYLA N. | 2022
MACFARLAND MIDDLE SCHOOL

I am sick of this reality
people ask my opinion I say neutrality
you choose people's personality by political decisions
but you don't know what they're truly like within
people say "be you"
but what is the point if you aren't too
so drawn by political pursuits
don't you realize we keep going in loops
every 4 years the presidency changes
new thoughts and new pages
even though some stay for eight years
there can be new thoughts and mindsets for their peers
can't you see
time goes on you cannot be stuck
on one thought one song
though I am only in the sixth grade
my words will not shatter or be dismayed
in fact it will get louder and prouder every day
I know my poem will be appreciated
such a young voice but so enunciated
now I shall send you off with this goodbye
and know I will not hesitate or be shy
I know this is a lot coming from an 11 year old
but all the kids out there need to be heard and be bold
so don't shut them down when they have a thought
they have to be embraced and taught
hopefully my words reached out to you today
goodbye to all and to all have a good day

THAT AIN'T GANGSTA

BY THE POET-ATHLETES FROM HOUSTON ELEMENTARY SCHOOL | 2022

Shooting and killing,
THAT AIN'T GANGSTA!
Robbing and stealing
THAT AIN'T GANGSTA!
WELLLLLL!!
What about all the rappers,
We hear in the streets,
Or At school starting beef!
THAT AIN'T GANGSTA!
GANG Bangin on the set
THAT AIN'T GANGSTA!
Tryna protect your rep
THAT AIN'T GANGSTA!
Pulling out a strap
THAT AIN'T GANGSTA!
Not having your brothers back
THAT AIN'T GANGSTA!

continued on page 56

continued from page 56

Holding down your fam
Now THAT'S GANGSTA
Not faking on TikTok or the Gram
THAT'S GANGSTA
Living to be old
Now THAT'S GANGSTA!
Standing up and being bold
THAT'S GANGSTA!
Self love and self care
Now THAT'S GANGSTA!
Spreading love & being fair
THAT'S GANGSTA!
Looking out for the youth
Now THAT'S GANGSTA!
Sticking to your code and being true
THAT'S GANGSTA!
WE ARE G.A.N.G.S.T.A.!
(Great Athletes Never Gonna Stop To Achieve)

BEING A GIRL

BY THE POET-ATHLETES FROM EXCEL ACADEMY | 2023

Being a girl is
Groundbreaking.
Like Simone Biles landing
a new trick that no one else can do.

Being a girl is
Warm.
Like the bowl of noodles
my mom makes me after school

Being a girl is
Helpful.
Like my auntie sitting
at the table doing homework with me

Being a girl is
Working hard.
Like my mom going
to her job every day.

Being a girl is
Sweet.
Like the Halloween candy
I share with my best friends.

continued on page 59

continued from page 58

Being a girl is
Creative.
Like me
when I pick out an outfit

Being a girl is
Caring.
Like my family checking
in on me after a hard day

Being a girl is
Like a tiger in a rainforest.
Patient, powerful, and beautiful

Being a girl is
Unique.
There's no one who can do it like me.

Being a girl is
Sisterhood.
Like a secret handshake
between just me and you

Being a girl is
Royalty.
I was born with a crown
and nobody can knock it down.

COURAGE

BY THE POET-ATHLETES FROM MARIE REED ELEMENTARY SCHOOL | 2023

Your skin isn't paper so don't cut it
Your body isn't a book so don't judge it
Your life isn't a movie so don't end it
Your face isn't a mask so don't cover it
Your happiness isn't an option so don't argue with it
Your sadness isn't a cover so don't hide it
You have value so don't degrade it

I love myself—Yo me amo
I care about myself—Me cuido
I respect myself—Me respeto
I encourage myself—Me animo
I value myself—Me valoro
I trust myself—Confío en mí

continued on page 60

continued from page 60

I can stand up for myself when people say bad things to me
I have a team behind me that will help me score a goal
I can do anything, so can you. I am great and so are you.
I have courage to not give up and keep going

I am happy—soy feliz
I am brave—soy valiente
I am love—soy amor
I am strong—soy fuerte
I am fearless—no tengo miedo
I believe in myself—creo en mí mismo

I am calm like the waves

I am as courageous as a tiger about to hunt
I am courageous like a lion about to protect
I am courageous like an eagle about to fly

CROWN

BY THE POET-ATHLETES FROM IMAGINE HOPE—LAMOND | 2019

I am black excellence
I am a king
I am beautiful and loved
I have a dream
I am magic wherever I go
it is good to be a king
I can conquer anything
I am building my empire
I am the king of the throne
I am royalty
I am worthy
I am the ruler of my destiny
I am legendary
I reign supreme
confidence is key
to young kings and queens
we are extraordinary
in life's play
light to the path
destiny please
guide our way

UNTITLED

BY THE POET-ATHLETES FROM
AMIDON-BOWEN ELEMENTARY SCHOOL | 2019

My hair ain't going nowhere.
These long locks that I bare.
Been growing my hair.
I am aware that people stare, I really don't CARE!!!
But I love my hair...
My Hair Ain't Going NOWHERE!!!
With its vibrant color, and don't forget those waves like the sea!!!
Those clippers better vroommmmm pass me.
My hair ain't going nowhere.
My hair expresses me! And who I am but Don't Judge Me!!!
My hair is kinky, curly, colored, beautiful and natural, you'll see!!!
At times my hair defines ME!!

LIKE

BY THE POET-ATHLETES FROM KIPP DC: AIM ACADEMY | 2024

The way I talk is not the way I walk, like me flying in the air like a hawk; like me loving myself and not understanding my heart; like my soul breaks and I'm falling apart' like if I'm running and I'm skipping the clock. Like the clock keeps ticking and never stops; like the world keeps spinning and never pops; like I'm causing a scene and and never calling the cops; like holding the phone and making a drop; like observing the world and end up shocked; like seeing the cops that did it but the crook never got caught.

Like; having a cart and never shopping; like seeing a mop and never stop to sop. Like; seeing a TikTok and it doesn't make the stock.

Now if you find that you've heard the work like a lot, then you may wanna know that this is our culture; like we can't ignore that this is like our story!

WE ARE

BY THE POET-ATHLETES FROM
SHIRLEY CHISHOLM ELEMENTARY SCHOOL | 2024

WE ARE
LEADERS
WE ARE
LEADERS
We are Shirley Chisholm elementary school.
Shirley Chisholm said
"You don't make progress by standing
on the sidelines, whimpering and complaining,
you make progress by implementing ideas"
You can make a change, create new ideas that are not the same
Instead of whimpering, thinking negative thoughts,
Get out of your head, be the boss.
You can accomplish anything you imagine,
believe in yourself, anything can happen.

WE ARE
CREATIVE
Shirley Chisholm said
"If they don't give you a seat at the table, bring in a folding chair"
If they don't let you play in the game,
You have to make your own game.
In this world we need to lift all voices,
We know the way to make good choices.
If we don't let people be included,
things go wrong, voices muted.
Everyone deserves an equal part,
nothing good comes when we're apart.

continued on page 66

continued from page 65

WE ARE
COURAGEOUS
Shirley Chisholm said
"Be as bold as the first man or woman to eat an oyster"
Stick to your goals like mold
Be fierce!
Don't be afraid, be very bold.
I can be brave and do hard things,
Like walking on a tight-rope
on the thinnest strings!

WE ARE
BOLD!
Shirley Chisholm said,
"I'd like them to say Shirley Chisholm had guts.
That's how I'd like to be remembered."
You are brave even if you don't believe it,
don't hide yourself, keep your personality a secret.
It's ok if you fail, learn from your mistakes
don't get angry or frustrated be calm like ripples on a lake
Even if you think you've fell behind,
remember who you are, clear your mind.

WE ARE
BRAVE!

POWER OF YOUR SMILE

BY JAIDEN R. | 2018
MINER ELEMENTARY SCHOOL

If a bird can fly
and if Beyoncé can sing,
then what can our smiles do?
Your smile is a powerful part of your personality.
Your smile is worth much more than anything in the world.
Your smile might not be perfect, but
your smile is powerful.
Just like my mother's beautiful smile,
that lights up a room like the sun.
Your smile is powerful enough to cure a stone heart.
If you see someone with a frown,
just go to that person with a smile,
to make them feel good inside and outside.
How powerful do you think your smile is now?
So everyone at this time, let's all smile and hug one another.

SHINING BRIGHT

BY THE POET-ATHLETES FROM POWELL ELEMENTARY SCHOOL | 2018

Shining bright
Above the green
Figuring out
Who I'm meant to be

We are all stars

Is it Messi? Or Marta?
I do not know
But in the game
I will show

We are all stars

Is it Barack Obama?
Or Sonia Sotomayor?
We will see
How I can be
A part of my community

We are all stars

These are the values
　we represent
Poise, perseverance, and respect
Powerful panther
Nothing else to expect

We are all stars

Shining bright
Above the green
I am living
Who I'm meant to be

COPS AND THE PEOPLE

BY DA'NIYA A. | 2018
SMOTHERS ELEMENTARY SCHOOL

Education is the key to life,
But they're changing the locks,
Shooting us around the block,
Shooting each other then talking about these cops,
They call us the United States,
But we more divided,
We smart enough to outsmart them,
Years of being enslaved,
And we still ain't trying to get our education,
We sell drugs and shoot each other,
Even kids and we still don't care,
Just around Kelly Miller two little girls got shot,
But we still gang bang,
Talking about are you blood or crip,
When y'all get shot y'all wanna say stuff about theses cops,
But this be our people,
All I gotta say is we can do better

KINDNESS IN THE WORLD

**BY THE POET-ATHLETES FROM
THOMSON ELEMENTARY SCHOOL | 2018**

Kindness in the world is low
We need to bring it up
When we……
Help people in need
Hold the door for the person behind us Spanish
Help our peers up when they fall
Help our neighbors with the laundry
Read a book to our little brothers and sisters
Stand up to bullies (not being a bystander)
Sit next to a friend that's alone at lunch
Help wash the dishes
Help our siblings with their homework
Keep our classroom clean
Make our friends laugh
Say thank you
Harper's concluding speech
This is how we show kindness
We need to bring it up

WE CAN INSPIRE

BY THE POET-ATHLETES FROM
TUBMAN ELEMENTARY SCHOOL | 2018

When you inspire me, and when I inspire you
Ooooh! There's nothing in the world that we can't do!
Cuando tú me inspiras, y cuando yo te inspiro
Oooooh! No hay nada en el mundo que no podemos hacer!

Beyoncé is hip hop royalty
Her moves are on fire
Her voice make me dance without fear
That's how she inspires!

Barack Obama is like the father of our country
He works to lift ALL of us higher
He won't stop trying until we're all equal
That's how he inspires!

My dad is like a shield
He works so hard he should retire
He's protective and dependable
That's how he inspires!

continued on page 72

continued from page 71

My teachers are the stars of my heart
There's so much I admire
They bring out my best every day
That's how they inspire!

My team is like a family
They run a soccer empire
When we make a mistake we learn from it,
That's how we inspire!

Sooooo…. When you inspire me, and when I inspire you
Ooooh! There's nothing in the world that we can't do!

BECOMING VISIONARIES

LET'S ALL SAVE THE WORLD TOGETHER

BY JASIA S. | 2011
BURRVILLE ELEMENTARY SCHOOL

Do you like nature?
Do you like playing outside?
Do you like hiking or watching the beach tides?

So Let's Save the World Together!

It's getting warmer nowadays
So don't let the hot weather carry you away.
Reuse, Recycle, Reduce and don't litter.
So tell this to relatives, friends and babysitters!

So let's save the world Together!

Go green, plant gardens, plant bushes or even a rose
And bring back that fresh natural smell to your nose.
Save electricity and cut off the lights and bring back those peaceful
    and cooler nights.
Don't waste the water we need to drink
So please don't let those precious drops go down the sink!

So Let's Save the World Together!

MY DREAM

BY JENNIFER P. | 2009
LINCOLN MIDDLE SCHOOL

My dream is to go to El Salvador
Because most of my parent's family is in Salvador
And I adore my family.

My dream is to be a pediatrician
Because I hate when babies get sick so I cure them
And give them their nutrition.

My dream is to make a goal
Because I want to hear my dad say, "Goooooal"
From the bleachers.

IN MY PERFECT WORLD...

BY XIU QI C. | 2011
THOMSON ELEMENTARY SCHOOL

In my perfect world...
My dreams become reality
Everything becomes surreal and bizarre
The animals dance and prance
The winters' snow becomes red
Buildings become as tall as Mount Everest
Though my perfect world might not be real,
It will always be my favorite and perfect world.

RECIPE FOR PEACE

BY THE POET-ATHLETES FROM
NOYES EDUCATION CAMPUS | 2009

Once there was a neighborhood that didn't get along
Friends fought friends even though they knew that was wrong
Then a bakery appeared with a recipe that made them break into song
The community finally had peace for long

Empty out a cup of bullies
Dump out a cup of fighting
Sprinkle in a bit of caring
Add a cup of sharing
Add a pound of respect
Add a cup of sportsmanship
Mix in a pound of compassion
And bake in a ton of love

The community ate and ate until they were so happy they couldn't eat anymore
They decided they should share with more!
Soon they filled the bellies of others with a piece of peace
Everyone across the world was happy
"Peace is for you and you and you," they said
Peace is nice!

THE SKY IS THE LIMIT

BY A'DORA W. | 2009
ARTS & TECHNOLOGY ACADEMY

The sky is the limit as to what I can do
with faith in God and self-confidence too,
I can be a female boxer like Laila Ali
or inspire others with my words
just wait and see!

Rosa Parks, Harriet Tubman, or Martin Luther King, Jr.
are just a few that stood up for their rights even though
    others didn't want them to!

I'm sure if they were here they would tell you they did
    what they had to do!
They had to make a change.... a difference too!
Trailblazing and paving the way for me and for you!

So I stand before you today full of hope
and a heart full of joy
because I know the sky is the limit as to what I can do!

In case you haven't heard, or perhaps you didn't see
Barack Hussein Obama
the first black president has made HISTORY
This proves that the SKY is truly limitless when it comes
    to me!!!!

I HAVE THE POTENTIAL

BY THE POET-ATHLETES FROM ARTS & TECHNOLOGY ACADEMY | 2010

I have the potential to be the BEST
But all you see are results on a test
The DC-CAS doesn't assess my true abilities
Provide me with a quality education and I'll achieve proficiency
I'm tired of teachers teaching to a test
Then we leave school and still don't measure up against the rest!
Let's buckle up and not settle for less
And work together to be the nation's best
In years to come you will hear and speak my name
In our nation's capital or on Hollywood's Walk of Fame
Remember.....I have the potential to be the BEST, but just know
that my worth is more than just the results on
some standardized test!

I WISH I WAS A WISHING WELL

BY KEIRY A. | 2021
BANCROFT ELEMENTARY SCHOOL

I wish I was a wishing well
So I could grant people's wishes

I wish I was a wishing well
So I could stop racism

I wish I was a wishing well
So people would stop throwing plastic
And other harmful stuff in the ocean

I wish I was a wishing well
So people would respect the LGBTQ community

I wish I was a wishing well
So I could stop global warming

I wish I was a wishing well
So I could make gun violence stop

I wish I was a wishing well
So the pandemic could come to an end

I know that there are many more problems with the world
But I wish I was a wishing well
So my generation and the future generations could have a better life

I WISH

BY ERIQ B. | 2011
ARTS & TECHNOLOGY ACADEMY

I wish the world was silent so I could be heard
I wish I was a star that has lots of hearts
I wish I were an outgoing person
I wish I was the loving thing that was filled with the
 spirit of a star so bright
I wish the world would not be so cold and dark
I wish the world would just have a loving heart

LET'S HAVE A FREE WORLD

BY MARSHAE J. | 2010
HOWARD ROAD ACADEMY

We live in a world full of bad things.
We go to bed looking and acting terrified.
We're scared while looking at the dark blue sky.
We're afraid, afraid of what's to come, we sit and wait.
Saying please, please don't let me die.
Crying for mercy.
We're frightened.
Help us out.
This is creepy.
Let us live.
Let us see the light.
All they say is "you might".

I'M DREAMING

BY THE POET-ATHLETES FROM BURRVILLE ELEMENTARY SCHOOL | 2021

I dream about being the best I can be.
I dream about not living on the street
I dream about being a champion
I dream about going to college (The Real HU)
I dream about my career and future
I am dreaming of the day I become a YouTuber, Nurse, Firefighter and a NBA Player
When the day is bright I know I am Right
Every person that Does Not Follow God's plan shall be brought to justice
And that's final
NO EXCUSES
I dream of giving speeches
Helping people around the world is my dream
So what you put into this world has a way of coming back you!
I will stand for what is right.
I AM A DREAMER!!!

THE POWER IN ME

BY THE POET-ATHLETES FROM
MARIE REED ELEMENTARY SCHOOL | 2021

I dream of being powerful.
I have big goals that are very, very possible.
I start to think about myself:
Am I truly smart? Am I a good person?
My mind is telling me to try, so I do and I keep going.
But there are no perfect days.
When you fly, there is always a fall.
I want to live my life. I deserve a good life.
Life is hard but you have to keep trying even if you think you can't.
Sometimes I'm sad. I don't like being mad.
Sometimes I don't know if I feel surprised or happy or nothing.
I fight the beast that is trying to break my mind.
When I know it is right, I use my might to fight.
I rise up in a surge of power,
The dark forces begin to cower.
I can do so many things no one else can do at all.

We are strong, not weak!
We are kind, not mean!
We are positive, not negative!
We are smart, not brainless!
We are bright, not dark!
Marie Reed has a spark!
We are powerful!!!

MY DREAM

SABA A. | 2010
MACFARLAND MIDDLE SCHOOL

My dream is to fly with pride
To sing with power
To feel the rain kiss my skin
To play soccer in muddy field
My dream is to design with passion
To soar through the clouds
To slide down a waterfall
My dream is to help with all my love

A RECIPE FOR A GREAT AMERICA

BY THE POET-ATHLETES FROM LASALLE-BACKUS EDUCATION CAMPUS | 2017

A recipe for a great America: Here's what we need:

Mountains of freedom.
24 gallons of gun control and fair immigration laws.
Bus loads of funding for education
A billion tons of brotherhood—stop deporting people!
15 acres of respect for our elders
Houses full of family love
Bundles of uncorrupt government officials
An infinity of GOOD LEADERSHIP!

Like me for president of the USA

Mix these ALL together
Sprinkle on some kindness and love
Serve this across the country
And we will have a great America

MY MAGICAL WORLD

BY ASHLEY R. | 2017
BANCROFT ELEMENTARY SCHOOL

My magical world is full of birds chirping
And flying around the sky.
The trees are made of cotton candy
And I will eat them all.
The sidewalk will be as white as vanilla.
I love the birds chirping, I love the song.
The grass will be as soft as a pillow.
The sidewalk will be as hard as a granola bar.
    Then smell will be sweet and sour.
That will be my magical world.

JUST IMAGINE

BY THE POET-ATHLETES FROM RAYMOND EDUCATION CAMPUS | 2019

Imagine a world free of homelessness
where kids grow up to be what they want to be
Just imagine
Imagine living in a world carefree and
living your life without the inequality
Just imagine
Imagine a world where cops were more patient and
living in a country without the lack of education
Just imagine
Imagine a world that wasn't so opinionated
And people who had dreams were able to make it
Just imagine
When you think of the world, what comes to mind?
Do you think of it for what it really is or
are you blinded by the lies?
Just imagine

MARKING THE FUTURE

BY THE POET-ATHLETES FROM BANCROFT ELEMENTARY SCHOOL | 2018

President Obama was the first African American
    president of the United States…
He left his mark

Malala fought for young girls' rights to go to school
She left her mark

Lincoln abolished slavery during a time when some
    believed slavery was ok…
He left his mark

Pele persevered when people told him that he was poor,
    black and he was never going to be a soccer player…
He left his mark

My parents work hard for me to have a good education
    and future…
They left their mark

My coaches work hard for us to learn every day…
They left their mark

Ruby Bridges ended segregation in schools…
She left her mark

Big or small, loud or quiet, all of us can make a change
    and leave a mark on the world

PEOPLE OF THE WORLD

BY THE POET-ATHLETES FROM
BEERS ELEMENTARY SCHOOL | 2018

Boys and girls, can we have your attention?
We need to make this world a better place for the next generation!
I know some people will not listen, but this is education!
First lose your assumptions, and then you can function without any hesitation!
Have a revelation and represent our great nation!
I have never seen so much hate and violation!
These people have no respect for this congregation!
Get over yourself, do right and make your children live up to the right expectations!

SAVING OUR GENERATION

BY THE POET-ATHLETES FROM IMAGINE HOPE—TOLSON | 2018

What will our generation be known for?

Oh Oh...I know: Orange Justice

Oh Oh...I know: Shoot Shoot Shoot

Naw Bruh, We need to Level up.

Level up...Level Up...Yeah, Level up to success.

Because I will help stop violence

I will help others in need

Through the leaves of the forest trees?
On top of the mountains? Or upon the grass below?
Where is it?

It's inside of me. We will be the change. You will be the change.

TOGETHER, we will change the world!

WE ARE THE FUTURE

BY THE POET-ATHLETES FROM SEATON ELEMENTARY SCHOOL | 2018

My friend over here might be the next president.
My friend over there might be the next soccer player
My friend in the crowd might be the next lawyer
I might even be the next Maya Angelou!

Did you know that we are the future?
When I look at this world I don't like what I see
So it's gonna be up to me
And you! And you! And you!

I think you know what to do

You might think you're never gonna be somebody
BUT, if you got a big dream
You work hard and study
You can, and you will
And get even better still!

You might think that you can't but YES YOU CAN!

YES WE CAN!

'Cause we are the future!
'Cause we are the what? "the future!"
We are the what? "the future!"
We are the what? "the future!"

DREAMS

BY THE POET-ATHLETES FROM WALKER JONES EDUCATION CAMPUS | 2018

When I dream, I dream in color
Big, bright, beautiful color
When I dream I dream in 3D
like I can touch it, it's right there
When I dream, I dream in HD
large and in charge, clear as day
When I dream, I dream in stereo
loud enough for all to hear
When I dream, I dream BIG
big enough for the world to see
Most importantly, WE DREAM
and when we believe it, we achieve it
Now I just have one question,
How do you dream?

AFTERWORD

BY CLINT SMITH

Last year, I attended my first ever DC SCORES Poetry Slam. When I arrived at the venue, the line to get into the event was around the corner. It was the sort of line you typically see for people waiting to get into a professional sporting event, or at a concert to see their favorite musician. "This line," I thought to myself, "is for an elementary school poetry event??" It was extraordinary.

The air was thick with anticipation and excitement. There were parents, neighbors, friends, and fellow students who had come here to cheer on their young poet as they stepped on stage—many for the first time—to represent their schools.

Inside, the energy was even more exhilarating. Children adorned in different colored shirts representing different schools, sang and chanted and danced as the DJ played some of their favorite songs. Two students from neighboring schools jumped in the middle of the aisle and had an impromptu dance contest as everyone around roared with elation and cheered them on. The energy of the space was pulsing through me, I might have done a little shoulder bop myself.

When the poems began, students came to the stage—school by school, poet by poet—and shared poems that reflected the fullness, complexity, and humanity of their lives. There were poems about the emotional impact of living in communities plagued with gun violence;

there were poems about experiencing racism at the hands of police and even sometimes within their schools; there were poems about losing family remembers to illness, and sometimes even to murder. But these poems were not only about trauma. There were also poems about so much more. There were also poems about the way that family and friends could provide a sanctuary of hope in times of economic despair; there were also poems about the joy they feel when going out on the field to play soccer with their friends; there were also poems about how much a group of young poets loved the mumbo sauce from their neighborhood eatery. All of these poems, together, painted a robust, beautiful, and honest picture of what life is like for so many of our young people growing up in Washington, DC. I left the poetry slam that night forever changed by their passion, their brilliance, and their bravery.

    The poems you've had the opportunity to spend time with in this anthology paint a similar picture of the multifaceted experience of our young people. So many of them have been through so much. They have lived through COVID-19, political turmoil, and economic instability. But they have also made friends, discovered new passions, and found their voices. These poems made me laugh, they made me cry, and they gave me the opportunity to see the DMV with new eyes.

    My life has been largely defined by the two elements that make DC SCORES what it is. I grew up with a soccer ball at my feet, playing the game competitively from Kindergarten all the way through college. In college, as my soccer career was winding down, I re-discovered a love for poetry that had begun when I was young. While I was still on the soccer team, I also started a poetry club on campus and began participating in local poetry slams and open mics in the area. Fast forward to today, and soccer is still a huge part of my life. I'm a diehard Arsenal fan (what an emotional roller coaster), a soccer dad to my two kids

(I'm basically their Uber driver), and even still play on occasion (when my knees allow it).

I also now make my living as a writer, and have published two books of poetry that have been read all over the world. I say all of this to say, when I see DC SCORES, I see myself. I see the sort of program I so desperately wish I would have had as a young person. It is a program that brings together two of the things I love most in the world—soccer and poetry—while adding the essential ingredient of community service. I know that, if there had been such a program in New Orleans in the 90s that it would have been transformative for me. It would have helped me realize—much earlier than I did—that being an athlete and being an artist were not mutually exclusive, but that they in fact could go hand-in-hand.

Today, as a member of the DC SCORES board, I have seen first-hand how this organization changes the lives of students, schools, and communities every day. And while the soccer-focused element of our programming often gets much of the attention, we should not forget—as this book shows—how integral the arts are to the core of what DC SCORES does.

Having all of these poems together in a single anthology now allows us to archive the first 30 years of DC SCORES poetry. It gives us a time capsule to hold and value and remember. Some of the poet-athletes in this book now have children of their own who may soon, or already do, participate in DC SCORES programs. Maybe they cheer on the same sidelines during a soccer game where someone once cheered for them. Maybe they clap from the same seats at the poetry slam where someone once clapped for them. What this does is show us the way that DC SCORES is creating an intergenerational lineage of poet-athletes across the region. It is these poet-athletes who will grow up to become adults using the lessons they learned during their time in DC SCORES to build a more just, more equitable, and better DMV.

I couldn't be prouder of the students, teachers, community members, supporters, and staff who make up this organization. I am so grateful for their tireless work and their generous spirits.

And I am so grateful to you, reader, for taking time with the work of these poet-athletes. Please share their poems with others and please support this incredible organization as it embarks on its *next* 30 years. I can't wait to see what's in store.

—CLINT SMITH

DC SCORES founder Julie Kennedy (back row, second from left) with girls in her Marie Reed Elementary School class, circa 1994.

Poet-athletes perform at DC SCORES' 2000 Poetry Slam.

Poet-athletes enjoying a DC SCORES game in the late 90s.

Poet-athletes compete in Jamboree, an annual DC SCORES soccer tournament, in 2002.

Poet-athletes pose in t-shirts commemorating DC SCORES' 10th anniversary in 2004.

A poet-athlete from Bancroft Elementary helps First Lady Michelle Obama harvest produce from the White House garden in 2009.

Poet-athletes pose at Fall Frenzy, DC SCORES' fall community festival, in 2014.

Poet-athletes in DC SCORES' Junior program play on the pitch at DC's Audi Field, 2019.

A poet-athlete awaits their turn on the mic at DC SCORES' Eastside Poetry Slam in 2017.

A poet-athlete delivers her solo poem at DC SCORES' Eastside Poetry Slam in 2022.

Members of the Brookland Middle School team prepare for their Capital Cup Championship game at Audi Field in 2023

A Junior SCORES poet-athlete on the mic at DC SCORES' Westside Poetry Slam in 2024.

ABOUT DC SCORES

DC SCORES empowers youth to lead healthy lives, be engaged students, and have the confidence and character to make a difference in the world.

We were founded by a DC public school teacher, and we are deeply invested in the neighborhoods where we work. We have faith in the power of young people to create change through sports, the arts, and service.

We create empowering spaces where youth show up as their full, authentic selves—all year long.

As the school year begins, poet-athletes form close-knit bonds with their soccer team and raise their voices on issues they care about through poetry workshops. In the spring, they continue to work together on and off the field by giving back to their community through service learning projects based on the themes explored in their poetry.

By working directly with and in schools, DC SCORES creates safe environments where young people can build connections with their community and become transformational youth leaders in their neighborhoods.

LEARN MORE AT DCSCORES.ORG

ABOUT SHOUT MOUSE PRESS

SHOUT MOUSE PRESS supports the creation and publication of diverse books by young people for young people. Our books and programs activate youth power, advance social justice, and expand representation in youth literature. The writers (ages 12+) we coach are underrepresented within young people's literature, and their perspectives underheard. Our work provides a platform for them to tell their own stories and, as published authors and public speakers, to act as leaders and agents of change.

SMP authors include immigrant, incarcerated, queer, Black, Muslim, Latinx, and otherwise marginalized youth in Greater Washington, DC. Their original children's books, novels, comics, memoirs, and poetry collections are inspired by their own lived experiences and engage readers of all backgrounds. With 50+ titles, 20+ book industry honors, and over 140,000+ books in circulation, Shout Mouse authors are proving that peer voices are powerful voices—and they need to be heard.

LEARN MORE AT SHOUTMOUSEPRESS.ORG

OTHER YOUNG ADULT TITLES FROM SHOUT MOUSE PRESS

How to Grow Up like Me, Ballou Story Project (2014)

Trinitoga: Stories of Life in a Roughed-Up, Tough-Love, No-Good Hood, Beacon House (2014)

Our Lives Matter, Ballou Story Project (2015)

The Untold Story of the Real Me: Young Voices from Prison, Free Minds Book Club & Writing Workshop (2016)

Humans of Ballou, Ballou Story Project (2016)

The Day Tajon Got Shot, Beacon House (2017)

Voces Sin Fronteras: Our Stories, Our Truths, Latin American Youth Center (2018)

I Am the Night Sky: ... & other reflections by Muslim American youth, Next Wave Muslim Initiative (2019)

The Ballou We Know, Ballou Story Project (2019)

They Called Me 299-359, Free Minds Book Club & Writing Workshop (2020)

When You Hear Me (You Hear Us), Free Minds Book Club & Writing Workshop (2021)

Black Boys Dreaming, Beacon House (2021)

What It Cost Us: Stories of Pandemic and Protest in DC (2023)

The Light Looks Like Me: Words on Love From Queer Youth (2025)

For the full catalog of Shout Mouse books, including illustrated children's books, visit **shoutmousepress.org**.

For bulk orders, educator inquiries, and nonprofit discounts: email **orders@shoutmousepress.org**.

Books are also available through Bookshop, Amazon, select bookstores, and select distributors, including Ingram, Follett, and Mackin.

www.ingramcontent.com/pod-product-compliance
Lightning Source LLC
Chambersburg PA
CBHW070151080526
44586CB00015B/1932